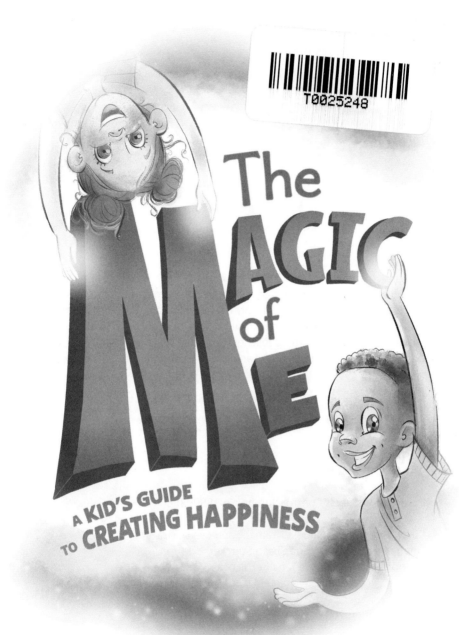

The MAGIC of ME

A KID'S GUIDE TO CREATING HAPPINESS

BECKY CUMMINGS

FREE KIDS PRESS

ISBN: 978-1-951597-24-5 (paperback)
ISBN: 978-1-951597-25-2 (e-book)

Library of Congress Control Number 2018909388

Cover design by Emanuela Ntamack and Eve DeGrie
Editing by Laura Boffa and Susan Strecker
Interior book design by Elena Reznikova

Second edition 2021.

Visit **www.authorbcummings.com**

Printed in the USA
Signature Book Printing, www.sbpbooks.com

Dedication

To my former square pegs who were perfectly shaped by God—Tim, Maya, Sierra and Mark. Thank you for being you. I'm blessed our paths crossed. As honored as I was to be your teacher, I'm more honored you were mine.

To my beautiful children Tyson, Calvin and Faith for opening my eyes and filling my heart. You gave me the drive to put my lessons on paper, so I can share my message with the world.

To my husband Jeff for always supporting me through the years as I learn, grow, and shift to new opportunities.

Table of Contents

Note to Kids

Dear Reader,

You are a magical, amazing person! You were created perfectly and everything about you is special. You have powers far beyond what you know. You are here right now on Earth to create your story!

My name is Becky Cummings. I am a mom of three kids, a teacher, a dancer, a world traveler, an animal lover, an artist, a writer . . . but most importantly I am your guide as you read through the pages of this book. You can read it in order or skip around to different chapters. You can ask a grownup for help or to read with you. If there is something you want to talk further about, please ask a grownup you trust. The more you discuss what you read the better you will understand it and use it in your life.

It is my hope this book will empower your mind and awaken your soul! May each chapter inspire you to be your best version and live the joy-filled life you deserve.

 With Love,
Ms. Becky

Part 1

You

Are

Loved

You Are a Masterpiece

What is a masterpiece? It can be a piece of art, a jaw-dropping building or some other creation so marvelous that people will travel all over the world just to see it. A masterpiece is amazing, valuable, rare, special and treasured — just like you! It is truly one of a kind. That is why you are a masterpiece! There is only one of you and there will only ever be one of you.

From the beautifully colored hair on your head to the shape of your toes, you are unique. All your features including your skin color, eye shape, eye color, hair texture, body shape and so much more were given to you. They create your body, which is like the cover of a magical book. This cover is meant to guard the most precious story inside . . . the story of you.

When you were created the universe smiled with joy. God made no mistakes and he planned for the beautiful creation that is now you. Do you know you came to this Earth at the perfect time? You are meant to be here now to do many great things during your life.

When you were born a few unique gifts were chosen to be part of you. Only you have this combination of special gifts. God hopes someday you will use these gifts to bring greatness to the world by sharing them with other people.

1. Have you ever seen a masterpiece before? If not, what masterpiece would you like to see? _____

_____

_____

_____

2. If you have seen a masterpiece before how did it make you feel? If you haven't, how do you imagine the masterpiece would make you feel? _____

_____

_____

_____

3. Look into the mirror and give yourself a compliment. Say, "I love you!" and thank yourself for being you. If you feel silly, it's okay. Repeat it each day — soon it won't feel so silly anymore!

You Are More
than a Body

We live in a physical world, which means we use our five senses to understand what is happening all around us. We see with our eyes, we hear with our ears, we smell with our noses, we taste with our tongues and we feel with our hands and skin. All of this information goes into our brains and helps us know what is going on. Sometimes our bodies are so good at using our senses that they trick us into believing that what we see, hear, smell, taste and feel is all that there is. But the truth is there is much more.

There is another part of you that is more powerful than your body. Close your eyes and picture a red, delicious apple. Can you see it? Could you describe what it looks like? Now in your head say the word "apple." Did you hear it? Although you didn't use your eyes or ears, you were able to see and hear. Pretty amazing, right? This other part of you that is super incredible is your mind. It is the part of you that cannot be seen or located. It is the part of you that is not physical or touchable. It's your connection to your spiritual side and it is said to be everlasting.

1. Describe a dream you had recently. How do you think you could see such vivid pictures without using your eyes?

    _____

    _____

    _____

    _____

    _____

    _____

    _____

2. Have you ever noticed you talk to yourself in your head? What are your thoughts right now?_____

    _____

    _____

    _____

    _____

    _____

    _____

    _____

Loving Your Body

*I*magine you have been given the most beautiful sports car as a present. It is your favorite color and style, it is in mint condition and it drives super fast. Your car can take you to any place you'd like to go. When you are inside the car, it is so much fun to drive. Also, imagine that you were told you would need to drive this car for the rest of your life. There would be no upgrades or trade-ins. This would be your only car!

How would you treat your car? Would you wash it often? Would you make sure the oil got changed and tune-ups happened regularly? Would you fill it with the best quality gas available? Would you keep the inside clean and organized? Most likely you would do these things. You would care for your car with all your heart knowing it had to last you a lifetime.

Your physical body is like your car. Your soul is like the driver inside. It operates your physical body and needs it to get around! You will only get one body for this lifetime. You get to decide how to treat it! Everything you do will have an effect on your body.

Many people actually take better care of their homes or cars than their bodies! This is a scary thought. It's really important to recognize how much our bodies allow us to enjoy life. Your beautiful body has amazing capabilities. But just like a car, it can break down and not work well if it is not given the proper care.

Sometimes we compare ourselves to others and get caught up on silly things. We might not like the color of our hair. We might feel too short or too tall. We might think we are too heavy or too skinny. It is easy to judge what we feel is wrong with our bodies. Instead, focus on all that is right! Love your body with all your heart and send it gratitude for all it can do.

We take for granted the little things our bodies do for us. It is only when we have a problem that we realize these little things are actually big and important. If we couldn't do them it would be life changing. It is an incredible experience to notice all our bodies can do. Thank your body if it allows you to walk. Thank your body if it allows you to talk. Thank your body if it allows you to see. Thank your body if it allows you to hear. The list of things your body can do goes on and on. Celebrate all these abilities and love your body.

When you are making choices about anything in life, ask yourself if it's good for your body! Pay attention to how certain foods, drinks, activities, people, and thoughts make you feel. Do more of what makes you feel good and healthy.

God made us each unique. Nobody has

ever looked exactly like you and no one ever will. Appreciate that you are one of a kind, irreplaceable and special. You have been gifted with a rock star vehicle to take you anywhere you'd like to go on this life journey. It is your job to keep your car beautiful and running well so it is in peak performance all the days of your life!

1. What are five things you can be thankful your body does?

2. What choices did you make today that helped your "car" feel and look its best?

3. Imagine what it would be like to only have the use of one hand. Wear a sock on your hand for a few hours or even a full day! Talk about your experience with a grownup or friend.

4. Blindfold yourself for a period of time such as 15 minutes. Make sure a grownup is with you for safety. Tell a grownup or friend about your experience.

You Were Given
Many Gifts

Everyone loves receiving gifts! Think back to a recent present you were given. How was it wrapped? How did you feel when you opened it? It's so exciting to be given a surprise and be filled with wonder about what's inside. You know the person giving it to you did so with love and that makes the present super special too.

When you open that gift, you probably feel joyful and excited. Maybe it's something you have always wanted and now your heart's hopes have been answered! Sometimes it's something you don't know much about. Then you can experience the adventure of exploring something new and unknown!

God loves you so much that he also gave you gifts the moment you were born. These gifts can't always be seen with the eyes, but they are always with you. For instance, think of a kid in class who is gifted at math. While the whole class might be trying to add basic numbers, she may be working on double-digit multiplication.

Other kids are gifted athletes and can catch a ball practically blindfolded! It's like they have hidden jetpacks in their sneakers and they can outrun a cheetah. Speaking of cheetahs, some kids are natural animal magnets and it seems all animals just want to be around them. You may find your gifts in any area of your life! You may find it easy to name what your gifts are, or you might have to think hard or try out different things to find them. But don't worry, God gave gifts to everyone!

Take a moment to think about what you love to do or learn about in your free time. This can help you identify some of your gifts. Maybe you like to draw, so perhaps you are a gifted artist. Maybe you like to learn about rocks and crystals, so perhaps you will learn how these can be used to heal people or create advanced technology. See the list below for more ideas, but keep in mind these are only a few.

I like . . .	my gift might be . . .
to sing	singer
to fix things	builder or inventor
to play sports	athlete
to help people	healer or teacher
to play outside	protector of nature
to paint	artist

Your gifts may turn into your hobby or even a future career. The great part is that you have several of them now and there are more to come. Explore each gift and learn about any topic that interests you.

As you get older you will be given additional gifts too! Be open to learning and trying new things all the time. I never took dance lessons as a child, but I started to take them in my twenties. After several years of practicing a little each week, I evolved into a gifted salsa dancer. I never imagined that would be an area I would be talented in since I didn't start until I was an adult. You will be surprised by all the presents God will gift you at the different stages of your life.

Always thank God for your current gifts and use them wisely. No one gives a gift and wants it to stay in the box. People give gifts with the

intention you will take it out, use it and enjoy it. God feels the same. When you use your gifts to bring joy to yourself and others, it makes God smile. Do not brag about your gift though, because that shows you are taking credit for it. Instead, thank your Creator and give the glory back to God. Being responsible with your gifts will bless you further. Soon your gifts will get stronger and new ones will appear.

1. What do you like to do or learn about?

_____

_____

_____

_____

_____

_____

_____

_____

_____

2. How might this be a gift for you?

_____

_____

_____

_____

_____

_____

_____

_____

3. How might you use this gift to help others?

_____

_____

_____

_____

_____

_____

_____

_____

4. Write yourself a few sticky notes about what you like about yourself. Stick them around your room to remind yourself about the gifts you have been given.

Some Gifts
Are for Others

Do you enjoy going to birthday parties? When I was younger I certainly did. We always celebrated at the birthday girl's house and played games like pin the tail on the donkey and drop the clothespin in the jar. Then we ate homemade cake and watched the birthday girl open her presents. That was always the hardest part for me. It seemed like the birthday girl would get everything on my wish list. I knew it was wrong to envy her presents, but it was so hard not to feel jealous.

Have you ever felt this way at a party? Did you watch with googly eyes as your friend or sibling tore open their presents with pure joy? It can be very challenging to watch other people get gifts you don't have.

There are times we feel jealousy or envy in our everyday lives too. When we notice other people's gifts from God, it hurts sometimes. You may look at your classmate and think, *Wow she is a great reader! Why can't I read like that?* Or maybe you see a friend's artwork and say to yourself, *How does he come up with those ideas?* When we witness other people's gifts it can sometimes make us feel like we aren't good enough. We tend to compare ourselves and discover that we can't do what someone else can do.

This is when we need to remember that God gave us all different gifts. Life would be so boring if we all had the same gifts or if we were talented at everything. We were meant to struggle in certain areas. There would be no challenge and opportunity to learn if we didn't.

When you see the gifts of friends and family members, God wants you to see His glory. Keep your thoughts and feelings positive by giving the person a compliment about their gift. This loving energy is stronger than the feelings of envy or jealousy. It will help to increase both of your gifts when you react with love. It's a win, win! God wants you to know all gifts come from one source, Him. God is abundant, which means He has plenty to give. You can work to strengthen your gifts and gain more. Be thankful for your gifts and you will continue to be blessed.

1. What gift (God given) does a friend have that you have wanted?_____

_____

_____

_____

_____

_____

2. What compliment can you give him or her?

_____

_____

_____

_____

_____

3. Start a gratitude journal. Take a blank notebook and at the beginning or end of the day write down a few things you are grateful for. It can be something specific to that day or something general in your life.

6

God Loves You

Think of the most amazing place you have ever been. Now pretend you are describing it to a friend who has never been there before. You can only pick one word. What word would you pick?

Do you think from your one word, your friend could understand your awesome place? If I were describing my favorite place, Disney World, I might use the word fun, exciting, amazing, unbelievable, or magical. But even though all of these words are true, there is no way one word could describe Disney. Even if you could describe Disney in one sentence or one paragraph, it still wouldn't be as good as the real thing. Our human words struggle to explain the awesomeness of Disney. It is just something you must experience to understand.

When I explain God, it's like trying to tell you about Disney World. I can give you a few words to tell you about God. But my words will never really give you the entire picture, because God's level of awesomeness can't be explained with human words.

As a human, I can only offer my own understanding to best define God, but keep in mind that there is not just one definition. It's always best to develop your own understanding by learning from many different sources. I do not believe that God is a person, but I will refer to God as "He and Him" in my explanation, just to make my words easier to understand.

God is the creator of the universe. I see God's work all around me; trees, mountains, clouds, elephants, birds and butterflies. Rainbows, thunder, lightning bugs, lily pads, waterfalls, cherry trees, spiders and sunsets. Snow, whales, newborn babies, flowers, wind and waves. The list is endless. Each day, take time to use your senses and be aware of your surroundings. When you see the world as God's creation, you can truly appreciate its beauty. Remember, God also created you as one of His masterpieces.

God is in spirit form. This means He is invisible but always present or around. Because God is always with us, everywhere, He is said to be omnipresent. If we think of God as a human, it would not make sense for Him to be everywhere all the time. But for the spirit of God, this is possible. The way a single fire can light many flames, all of us were created from the spirit of God and therefore we all have the spirit of God within us. God is everywhere and part of everything.

Since this is such a challenging thought for our human minds to grasp, I believe God did something extraordinary to help us connect with Him. According to the Bible, an ancient holy book, God wanted us to know Him on a personal level. So He put on his human suit and came to Earth and in the form of a person called Jesus. He started out as a baby and had the whole human experience. While Jesus was here on Earth, he led a life devoted to loving and serving others. Jesus taught people how to lead good lives, healed the sick and ultimately died for his beliefs.

While Jesus was on Earth, he explained to us that God is our Father, creator of everything! A heavenly father who loves us unconditionally, no matter what we do. He is a father who forgives us, even if we do wrong or sin. He is a father who loves us so much that He gave us free will. This means we have the ability to make our own choices. Jesus showed us that we could have a personal relationship with God and talk to Him directly when we pray.

Have you ever used prayer to talk to God? Anyone can do it. Here are some tips that might help you.

10 Tips for Praying

1. There is no one right way to pray, so don't feel stressed about how you do it. It's more important that you just do it.

2. You can pray alone during a quiet time, like first thing in the morning or before you go to bed.

3. You can pray with other people before you eat or when you need help.

4. You can say your prayer out loud or think it in your head.

5. You can pray for as long as you'd like and as often as you'd like.

6. You can pray anywhere.

7. You can thank God for being the ultimate creator and provider and share with Him what are grateful for in your life.

8. You can ask God to forgive you for anything. You can ask God to help you forgive others.

9. You can ask God for what you need or want. Remember, God hears all prayers but may not answer all of your requests. Just as your parents wouldn't give you everything you want because they know that it might not always be in your best interest, God responds the same.

10. You can pray for other people, by asking God to bless them with what they may need or want in their lives.

If I was asked to describe God in one word, I'd say God is LOVE. There is a deep love within you and that is the spirit of God. The way to honor God is to love yourself, love others, and love Him with all your heart.

1. How would you explain God to someone?

_____

_____

_____

_____

_____

_____

2. Tell about something you might ask for in your prayers._____

_____

_____

_____

_____

_____

_____

_____

_____

Part 2

Your Super Powers

Your Mind Is a Garden

*Y*our mind is an endless open field with rich soil that is ready for planting. You are the farmer. Your job is to choose which seeds will be planted to grow in your garden. You can plant anything you would like. Will you plant apple trees that will produce tasty fruit? Will you plant flowers that will blossom with vibrant colors and feed the birds and bees? Perhaps you will plant weeds that spread like crazy and destroy all the helpful plants? Yikes! That last idea seems so silly. Who would want weeds to grow and destroy the good plants in their garden? Nobody wants weeds, but they can pop up and take over if you don't tend to your garden.

The thoughts we think in our minds are like seeds. They can be good, bad or neutral. Many times they just happen naturally. But the more you become aware of your thoughts, the more control you can have over them. When you have a thought and recognize it's a bad one, you can choose to replace it with a positive one.

For example, if you got a low grade on your math test you might think, *I am horrible at math*. Weed alert! Thinking like this will only plant seeds in your mind that cause you to do poorly in math. Instead, change your thought to, *I am working hard to improve in math and learned new things through this test*. Planting this beautiful flower seed will really help you to learn and improve.

The more you practice planting positive thoughts, the better you will get at it. Your feelings are a great tool to help you recognize your thoughts. When you are feeling bad, pause to ask yourself why. Ask, "What thought(s) am I having that are causing these bad feelings? Can I change my thought(s) to be neutral or positive?" If you find yourself coming back to that bad thought, try to keep replacing it with the positive one you purposely created. When you do this, you are weeding your garden. You are making more room for the good stuff to grow.

1. Explain a time today when you felt a bad feeling like anger or jealousy._____

_____

_____

_____

_____

2. What thought did you have?

_____

_____

_____

_____

_____

3. What thought could you have instead to plant a flower seed? _____

_____

_____

_____

_____

_____

Your Thoughts Have Power

*D*o you remember the joy you felt when you first played with magnets? Do you remember wondering if they were magic? You could spend hours making them miraculously move. It was so fascinating to see how one magnet could push away from another. But when you turned it around, the magnet would fly towards the other magnet and connect. The bigger the magnets you had, the stronger connection between them.

Now imagine your thoughts are like mini magnetic laser beams of light that pour out of your head. Every time you have a thought you shoot one of these magnetic beams of energy into the world. Your thought goes off searching for a partner. It wants to connect with an energetic match and pull it in. Your thoughts are so powerful they have the ability to create your reality. This cool phenomenon is what people have named the Law of Attraction. They call it a law because it is always true. The attraction part means coming together. Whatever you focus on, you will draw to you. Therefore, it's important to keep your thoughts positive and focused on what you want in life!

When I was about nine I used the Law of Attraction to win a contest, even though I hadn't been taught about the Law of Attraction yet. I had recently won a doll at a local garden store as a raffle prize. Many people had bought tickets to win the doll and my ticket got picked. I was so excited.

A few weeks later, there was another raffle at my local McDonald's for a super-sized Snoopy dog that was about the same height as an adult. Since I won the last contest, I assumed I would win this one, too. My mother tried to prepare me for disappointment and explained that it was a totally different raffle that anyone could win. But I was completely confident that Snoopy would be mine. Sure enough, on the day of the raffle we got a phone call that the ticket with my name had been picked. I was thrilled to have my new stuffed animal that took up an entire seat in the car! I'm not so sure my mother felt the same way.

Later as an adult, I read many books about the Law of Attraction. I realized I had the power to bring good or bad things into my life, depending on what I focused on. So, I changed my thinking to bring more of what I wanted into my life. From a wedding on the beach, to adopting a baby and soon moving into my dream home, the Law of Attraction has been working well for me on my adult journey.

You can begin to attract what you want, too. Do you want to make the soccer team, adopt a pet or get an A in math? Whatever your goals and desires may be, you can begin to make them appear in your life!

It begins with changing your thoughts. You need to be very clear and focused on what you want. Then you need to think about your goal in a positive way as if you already have it or have done it. For example, let's say you are going to try out for the soccer team next month and you want to get on the team. Your first job is to keep all your thoughts positive and clean up any that are not helpful to you. If you think it's too tricky to make the team, instead think, *I am a strong and talented soccer player.* Then think as if your goal has already happened, *I am on the soccer team and my skills are valuable.*

To make this process more powerful here are five things you can do . . .

Adding Power to the Process

1) THINK IT

As you just learned, it starts with your thoughts. Spend time every day practicing thinking your positive thoughts, which can be called intentions. In the morning when you first wake up or before you go to bed are great times when your mind is quiet and ready. Just five minutes is perfect to start.

I am a strong and talented soccer player. I am on the soccer team and my skills are valuable.

2) SAY IT

Say your positive thoughts aloud with emotion and confidence that the universe is on your side.

"I am a strong and talented soccer player."

3) WRITE IT

Write down your intentions and place them where you can see them and read them throughout the day if possible. Sticky notes are great to use and can be stuck on a bathroom mirror, fridge, desk or bedside table.

I am a strong and talented soccer player.

I am on the soccer team and my skills are valuable.

4) PICTURE IT

Picture in your head what your intention would look like in real life. *For example, if you wanted to be on the soccer team, picture yourself in your soccer uniform running down the field and kicking the ball into the net for a goal.*

5) FEEL IT

As you are picturing your intention, feel it at the same time. Let your body get flooded with wonderful emotions. *For example, experience the adrenaline rush as your team cheers for you and gives you high fives. Add as much detail to this movie in your mind as you like. The more real and emotional you make it, the stronger your magnets will become!*

Once you realize the power of your thoughts you will understand the importance of staying positive and focused on what you want. You can use your mind to create the world you want. What you believe you will receive!

I am a strong and talented soccer player.

1. What is one goal you have in the near future?_____

_____

_____

_____

_____

2. What are some positive intentions you could say and write down to help you attract that goal into your life? Start with the words, "I am . . ."_____

_____

_____

_____

_____

_____

_____

_____

3. What can you picture in your mind and feel in your heart to strengthen your powers to attract that goal?_____

_____

_____

_____

_____

_____

_____

4. Create a vision board. Use magazines, the Internet or other resources to collect pictures that represent your future goals. Arrange them on a poster so it looks pleasing to you. Write down positive statements on your board that start with, "I am . . ."

Your Words
Have Power

What is the best compliment you have ever gotten? Wasn't it amazing that a few words from another person could be so powerful! They may have flooded your body with happy emotions and brought intense joy to your heart. On the other hand, can you remember a time when someone said something hurtful to you? Again, perhaps only a few words were spoken, but your body may have still been flooded with emotions. Only this time it was probably sad ones and your heart felt broken. Our words have incredible power, just like our thoughts.

While thoughts shoot out laser beams of energy from your head, your words are doing the same from your mouth. Everything you say contains energy that affects yourself and others. You just recalled how a compliment versus a put-down made you feel.

Imagine that when you talk to others your words can pour out of your mouth as either fairy dust or dirty oil. Loving and positive words that honor others are like fairy dust. They make people feel special, magical and empower them to be the best version of themselves. Hateful or negative words are like an oil spill. They pollute the area and cause lots of harm. When you attempt to clean up after an oil spill, it's really hard to remove all of the oil. Some damage will always remain. Hurtful words are hard to take back. That is why you have to watch what you say to others very carefully.

Not only do you have to monitor the way you speak to others, but you have to be mindful of how you speak about yourself and your own life. If you spend your time complaining, it is like taking a bath in your own oil spill. Your thoughts that lead to your complaints are probably negative too. Remember that what you focus on you will attract into your life. Instead of complaining about the negative, look for the positive and speak about that! Here are a few examples of how to change your oil spills to fairy dust.

Oil Spill	Fairy Dust
I hate cleaning my room.	I love how enjoyable it is to be in my room once it's clean.
Math is so hard!	Challenges in school give me a chance to grow and become smarter.
I don't like what is for dinner.	I am so blessed to have a meal to eat tonight.
I'm having a bad day.	I'm having a rough moment in a good day. I know it will pass.

When you start to sprinkle more fairy dust from your mouth you will see that it has a positive effect on everything. You will feel happier and draw more of what you want into your life. God gave you a mighty tongue! Do not let it be used like a sword to battle others. Instead, use it to bring wisdom and blessings to all.

1. What is one complaint you say often that is spilling oil into your life?_____

_____

_____

_____

_____

2. How can you reword it and change it into fairy dust?

_____

_____

_____

_____

_____

_____

_____

3. Set up an experiment with two seeds of the same kind from the same packet.

    → Plant them in separate containers and keep everything exactly the same. Make sure they get the same amount of water and sunlight from the same location. The only difference is the words you speak.

    → To one speak loving words telling the plant it is loved, beautiful, and special. To the other say mean words telling it that nobody loves it and it's ugly.

    → Repeat this daily and observe how your plants grow. Share your observations with others.

Your Actions
Have Power

What an amazing world it would be if we could use only our thoughts and words to make things magically appear. We could sit on the couch and just think our way to becoming a millionaire. Dream house, *poof*! Big old pool with a slide, *bam*! Unlimited sundae bar by the hot tub, now we're talking! Okay, so this is not going to happen. Unfortunately, the universe wants a bit more from you. There is a third and final piece of the puzzle which creates our super power triangle. Your final super power is the action you choose to take.

Action is what you choose to do that will propel you toward your goals and dreams. If you decide to climb Mount Everest, the world's tallest mountain, you must start with one single step. Then another and another, and so on. Each small step will get you closer to your goal. Eventually, you will reach the top of the mountain. The biggest factor of reaching the top is to just keep going. Never give up, even if you stumble and fall back a few steps. Like climbing a mountain, reaching every goal and dream you have means taking these small positive action steps. You will eventually get to your destination!

Here is the good news. You don't need to know exactly how to get there. It's okay to not have a perfect road map of every action you need to take to reach your goals. It's more important that you do something! Baby steps in the right direction will eventually get you there.

Have you ever left your house in the fog before? You know you need to go somewhere and it's a bit far away, but you can barely see in front of you. As your grownup drives the car forward you see just a little and you can keep going. The car continues to move forward slowly, and you see just enough to know you are headed in the right direction. Finally, you reach your destination. You don't need to see the whole path. You just need to trust you will arrive at your destination by moving along one step at a time.

If you use your two other super powers to keep your thoughts and words positive, it will help your actions move in a positive direction, too. For example, let's say you want to make the soccer team. You just learned what thoughts and words you need. So you think, *I am a great player and I'm on the team*. You visualize yourself on the team and say things like, "I am on the team, I'm playing my favorite position." Now, don't go sit on your couch and play video games. You won't be able to activate your super powers to their maximum ability. Allow your thoughts and words to motivate you to take some positive action. Now that you're feeling good, you may decide to practice each day until tryouts. This is an action to help you make your dreams come true!

Below is a triangle where each point is labeled. Any way you move around the triangle you can see everything is connected. If you think positive about something, you will speak positively about it which will lead you to taking positive actions. Positive actions will make you think positively about it and talk positively about it. This will make you want to take further positive actions. This can also work against you if you are negative. Your feelings can act like a thermometer to help you be aware of how your super power triangle is working. When any bad feelings like anger, jealousy, or sadness arise in you, check to see what you are thinking, saying or doing. Fix any of these areas and you will begin to notice improvements.

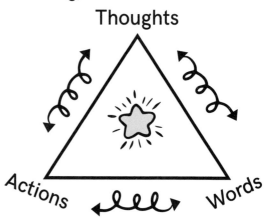

Here are a few examples of how I use the triangle in my life. The other day I was feeling a bit grumpy, so I tuned in to myself to see what was going on. I was thinking about how I felt tired and sick. I reviewed my actions. I had eaten several slices of pizza a few hours earlier. This helped me realize that when I eat pizza I don't feel good after. Next time I can take a different action, such as choosing a different food, eating less pizza, or eating it less frequently.

When I was in the process of writing this book, I had much information to share and a lot of chapters to write. I decided to take positive action by working on two chapters a week. I set aside time two days a week and worked on a chapter each day. I trusted I would have the right words to say as I started each new chapter. I wasn't sure how this book would get into your hands, because I couldn't see through the fog. I just used my super powers to keep my thoughts, words and actions positive. I told myself, "I am an author. You are reading my book and learning from it." And like magic, it happened!

1. What is one goal you have for the near future you'd like to achieve?_____

_____

_____

_____

_____

_____

_____

2. What actions can you take to help you manifest it, or bring it into your life?

_____

_____

_____

_____

_____

_____

_____

_____

_____

3. Why do you think it's important to not give up if you don't reach your goal right away?

_____

_____

_____

4. Write down a goal you want to accomplish in the next month. Then break down some action steps you can take to start working toward it. Make them specific which means write down exactly what you will do, how long and how often you will do it.

_____

_____

_____

_____

_____

_____

_____

_____

You Can Only
Control You

*D*o you have a chore you dread? I used to hate folding laundry. Washing clothes for a family of five, including three messy little kids, got overwhelming. By the end of the week, I would dump all the clothes on the floor and create Mt. Laundry. It was quite the sight. The kids would run and jump into it like a leaf pile. Although fun for them, I knew what it meant for me. I had hours of folding to do. Ugh, how boring! I'd complain to my friends, family, or even strangers about the horrors of laundry folding.

Then one day I decided to play some YouTube videos while I folded. I chose one that explained how to lift weights, a new interest of mine. I could listen while folding and do one of my favorite things, learn! Soon enough I did this each week. Any new topic I wanted to explore, I would find some related videos and play them while I tackled Mt. Laundry. Pretty soon I began to look forward to my chore! It became a relaxing few hours of my week that I enjoyed.

I realized that I was going to have to get the laundry done whether I liked it or not. It was much easier to find a way to like it, than to always approach it with dread. I learned there are many things in life I can't control. They may seem or feel bad. I also realized I could control my reaction to these things. This could make my experience much better!

You may have heard the expression, "When life hands you lemons make lemonade!" This silly expression is all about your response or reaction. Life will hand you lemons that are sour and bitter, not good to eat alone. You can take those lemons and make lemonade, which is sweet and lovely.

Our response is a choice and it is the key to how things will turn out. If you want things to be good, then react positively. Here is a scenario. You were supposed to go to a party, but you're sick and need to stay home.

Do you . . .

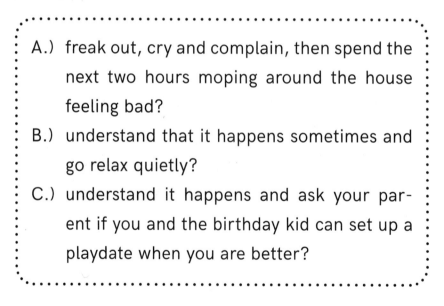

A.) freak out, cry and complain, then spend the next two hours moping around the house feeling bad?

B.) understand that it happens sometimes and go relax quietly?

C.) understand it happens and ask your parent if you and the birthday kid can set up a playdate when you are better?

In all three situations you are sick and can't control that you are missing the party. Your reaction will determine how you feel for the rest of the day. You actually get to choose your response! Now that is an advanced super power.

This does takes some practice. Most of the time we respond automatically without much thought. That usually leads to trouble. When you feel yourself getting upset, your first job is to be aware of these feelings. Then you can work to calm yourself down.

Take some deep, slow breaths. Counting to twenty can help you relax, too. When you are in a calmer state you can make better choices. You may feel hurt, upset, or angry. It is okay to allow these feeling to come, but then you can send them on their way. See if you can adjust your thoughts to be more positive. This will start to help your feelings too. It's okay to voice your feelings and then move on. I recommend using an "I statement" if you're talking to another person. An "I statement" goes like this:

I feel _____

when (you) _____

so (can you) please_____.

Let's say your little brother wrecked the art project you brought home from school. In the seconds after, you may want to punch him in the nose, but that won't lead to a good outcome. Instead, you use your breath and counting to calm down. Then you say, "I feel terrible when you wreck my project I worked so hard on, so please do not touch my projects anymore." The art is gone, so now you can choose to feel sad and complain. Or you can choose to let it go and be thankful you were able to create something so cool.

It can be very challenging to be positive when bad things happen. The more you practice, the easier it will get. You will also notice how much better it feels to respond with love, kindness, patience and forgiveness. So when you are handed a bunch of lemons, remember that God put you in charge of your own lemonade stand. He wants you to make your life sweet and wonderful. You have that choice and are responsible for your life!

1. What is something bad that happened to you this week?_____

_____

_____

_____

2. How did you react? Do you think you had lemons or lemonade?

_____

_____

_____

_____

3. If you had lemons, how could you turn them into lemonade? _____

_____

_____

_____

_____

_____

_____

Connecting to Your Super Powers

Are you ready to unleash your inner beast? Unlock your secret powers and become unstoppable! How do you activate all these super powers to live your best life? The greatest way to get to the next level of awesomeness is to sit in silence and think of nothing. Say what! Doesn't that sound a bit crazy, a bit bizarre? It's actually much harder to do than you think. I dare you to try it for just one minute. Close your eyes and sit without talking and think of nothing. If a thought pops into your head, ask it to nicely "head out" and start again. Go ahead and give it a try now.

Could you do it for a minute? It is very challenging and takes practice, so don't be discouraged! Most of us have a monkey mind that likes to jump around from thought to thought. All these thoughts can be very distracting and block us from connecting to our spiritual side. This is the part of us that we can't see that is said to be everlasting. Learning to calm your mind is a skill, just like learning to ride a bike or read. You will probably stink at first, but with time, patience and practice, you will get better. When you are able to quiet your mind completely and be in a peaceful state, this is called meditation. It's the key to unlocking your super powers!

There are many ways to meditate, so try them all and see what works for you. When you first begin meditating, it's okay to start with just a few minutes. Later you can gradually increase your time. You may want to try it first thing in the morning or right before bed. Here is a guide for basic meditation.

5 Steps To Meditate

1. Find a room where your dog won't lick you on the face or your little brother can't poke you in the eye. Sit on the floor cross-legged or lie down comfortably and close your eyes.

2. Open your hands so your palms are face up to the ceiling.

3. Focus on becoming aware of your breath. Notice how it is flowing in and out of your body. Then, close your mouth and breathe in slowly and deeply through your nose. Feel the air as it makes its way in, eventually making your belly expand. Then breathe out slowly letting all the air out.

4. Repeat this slow, steady breathing until you feel relaxed. Now stop thinking about your breath and just allow your body to relax.

5. Let your mind become blank. If thoughts pop in, which they will, just let them flow out and go back to relaxing.

There are many ways to meditate so experiment! Some people start off their meditation with a prayer or intention. They may ask a question or picture something they want to attract into their life. Many people listen to relaxing music of nature sounds or beautiful harmonies. Other people listen to a recording of someone talking and leading them through a meditation. This is called guided meditation. Many times, the person talking will encourage you to journey to a beautiful place using your imagination. Some people say a mantra, which is repeating a few words, as they breathe. This keeps the monkey mind busy so the

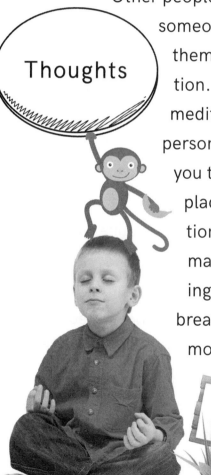

Thoughts

Shh . . .
Mind
Resting

person can relax. "I breathe in love, I breathe out worry," could be one you try.

If you're not ready to sit in stillness at home, you can try to meditate as you walk. You can do this at a park or with a grownup. Surround yourself in nature if you can and be silent as you walk. Focus on your breathing and just soak in your surroundings.

Once you get into the habit of meditating you will begin to experience some cool stuff! Everyone has different experiences. When I first started meditating I saw vivid colors with my eyes closed, especially purple. Sometimes I saw rainbows or heard birds singing. My hands and feet would get tingly and feel like they were melting into the air.

Each person's journey is unique. The important part is that you are open-minded about trying it. If you feel silly doing it, just know that people have been meditating since the beginning of time! Meditation is powerful. Quiet your mind and unlock your super powers. When you turn inwards for wisdom, you become unstoppable!

1. Do you know anybody that meditates? If so, ask them to share what they do.

   _____

   _____

   _____

   _____

2. What is one of the suggested ways you would like to try?_____

   _____

   _____

   _____

   _____

   _____

   _____

3. With an adult's guidance, go on the Internet and do a video search for children's meditation. See if there are any that interest you. Try one out!

The Power of Now

Try not to concern yourself with the past or the future. There is only now. If you think about tomorrow, when it arrives, it is no longer the future. It is now. When you think about yesterday, you didn't experience it as the past, you experienced it as right now. If you always exist in the NOW, it's important to keep your energy in the now and make the most of it!

When I was younger I used to worry a lot about the future. For example, whenever I went to a new grade I was worried I wouldn't understand what the teacher expected me to learn.

Also, I was always worried before a field trip that nobody would sit with me on the bus. So much of what we worry about never even occurs. We waste tons of energy and create lots of stress on our bodies for no reason!

Most of the time our now is pretty good. Check in with yourself now. Right at this moment are you okay? I meant at this exact moment, not in five minutes or later tonight. You probably will agree that you are in a good place. Most of the time we are doing great right now, but we are so caught up in the story of the future or the past that we can't even enjoy the present moment of now.

Imagine if we could always keep our attention in the present moment. How much more would we enjoy life? Right now I can hear birds chirping, the sun is beaming onto the flowers on my deck and my neighbor is cutting his grass. I am typing this chapter, which means I am sharing my messages with the world through books. That brings me happiness. My now is amazing. If I start to think about my to-do list or drift off to past thoughts, very quickly I will be pulled away from this beautiful present moment.

So I invite you to pause. Take a deep breath and check in to your now. If you do not like your current now, can you change it? Do you need to refocus your thoughts or change your actions? Sometimes as children you have less control over your now because you are in your parent's or guardian's home and need to follow the rules. As you get older this will change. You can choose your thoughts and actions to improve your now. The power to change your NOW lies within you.

My son was walking around with a grumpy face this morning. I asked him what was wrong. He told me he was in a bad mood because he didn't want oatmeal for breakfast since he ate it for dinner the night before. I simply reminded him that he could change his thoughts to be grateful that he had a hot breakfast that was healthy. Choosing a more positive thought could lift his mood. He could be happy right now.

The present moment is like a beautiful treasure box hidden at the bottom of the dark murky ocean. It is so easy to become distracted in the water and lose focus. But you must seek out that treasure! You hold the key to that box. Open it to reveal the treasure inside.

1. How is your now?_____
   _____
   _____
   _____
   _____
   _____
   _____
   _____

2. What could you do or think to improve
   your now?_____
   _____
   _____
   _____
   _____
   _____
   _____
   _____
   _____

Part 3

Loving
Yourself

You Can Heal Yourself

*H*ave you ever fallen off a bike or bumped into a table? I'm sure you could tell a good story about a time you got a nasty cut, scrape or broken bone! Most of us have a few exciting injury stories to share. But what we forget to tell is the most incredible part of the injury. This is the part after the accident when your body immediately responds and starts to fix itself. Think about how amazing that is. Your body is so smart that it knows how to heal itself.

Whenever you get sick, your body goes into combat mode. It sends little cells that are like fighters into the correct area of your body to battle whatever bacteria or virus is causing the illness. You may have experienced a fever before. Most fevers are actually great as long as they stay at a safe level. A fever is your body's way of turning up the heat to kill off anything inside you that does not belong. You can help your body work its magic by drinking extra water, resting and avoiding sugar. It's best to stay as natural as possible.

When we get a cut, it usually only takes a few minutes for the bleeding to stop. That is because our bodies make a natural bandage to keep our blood in. Special cells are also sent to the area to help fight off any possible infections. The body will make a scab to keep out yucky invaders that don't belong and grow some new skin over the next few days.

It's pretty impressive how your body knows what to do. Your heart beats on its own, your lungs keep air moving throughout your body, your stomach digests food and expels what is not needed and your body repairs itself. It does all these things on its own. Your body works the way it does because that's how God created you. But it is up to you to take care of your body.

It's very important to understand that God gave you free will. That means you can make choices in your life. Your choices will affect how your body works. Some of these choices involve what you eat and drink, how well you sleep, how you spend your time and how you think. Your choices can improve your ability to heal and be healthy or they can make you sick. The consequences of your choices may show up immediately, or they might show up later in life. You play a huge role in creating and maintaining a healthy body. God gave you an incredible body. There is healing power within you and your choices can strengthen it!

1. What is one time you had a bad illness or injury?_____

_____

_____

_____

_____

_____

2. Did you heal from it? How do you know you healed?

_____

_____

_____

_____

_____

_____

_____

_____

Food Is Medicine

*Y*our body is actually made up of the food you put in it. That hot dog you eat is going to turn into your hair, skin, blood and more. That apple you eat will become your eyes, nails, lungs and more. Almost everything you put in your mouth will eventually become your body.

This is because all the food you eat is always being used to build and repair your body. Your digestive system carefully breaks your food down to get to the nutrients it needs. Then your body uses these nutrients to build cells and repair itself if it's injured or sick. Cells are the basic units of life. They are so tiny that you can only see them with a microscope. Even though they are small, they are mighty and do very specific jobs in the body. For example, the cells that make up your heart, cardiac cells, contract and keep your heart beating about 52 to 115 beats per minute. Cells even multiply by producing exact copies of themselves. This is good because eventually they die, and new ones must replace them. You can see this when you trim your fingernails and notice after a few days they have grown. New nail cells are made and push old ones forward, making them longer.

The food choices you make are so important for you to build a healthy and strong body. You can give your cells super powers or make them super sick just depending on the fuel you feed them. You only get one body for this Earth journey, so you need to choose the best foods you can to fuel it!

The best food on the planet is anything that grows directly from the earth. Fruits and vegetables are your power foods. They provide the body with many of the nutrients it needs. It's smart to eat a variety of fruits and vegetables. Try to taste the rainbow by eating all the colors, which will help you get different vitamins and minerals.

In an ideal world, we would all grow our own produce in our organic gardens. Since this is not an option for most people, another idea is to support local farms, instead of large grocery stores. The less the food is handled the better. It's best to look for organic fruits and vegetables. This means they are grown naturally and not sprayed with any poisons to keep insects and critters off.

A great way to sneak in some of these fruits and vegetables is to pack them for school. An apple, a banana, a bag of grapes, sliced cucumbers or peppers are easy snacks to bring. Add a side of hummus or nut butter for dipping to change it up.

Just as some foods can make your cells sing with joy, others can make you feel sick or feed an illness in your body. Some food companies have tried to gain more money in a sneaky way. They make their products taste yummier by adding extra sugar, fake flavors, or other ingredients that are not natural. Our mouths may enjoy the taste, but they make our cells sick. Learn to look at food labels and watch out for ingredients you don't recognize. If you can't say the name of the ingredient or a grownup can't explain what it is, then it's probably best to not eat it.

The chart at the end of this chapter shows 25 commonly eaten foods separated into two groups: healthy choices and foods to limit or avoid. You will notice animal meat and animal products such as yogurt are listed as food to limit or avoid. This is a highly debatable subject. I put animal products there for several reasons. First, I feel compassion for all animals. They deserve to live a happy life. The earth provides enough other foods to consume. Second, raising animals for meat requires an insane amount of water and grains. We could greatly reduce world hunger if we fed these grains directly to humans, instead of animals being raised for meat. Finally, there is much research showing that eating mainly plants and fruits keeps you super healthy.

Remember, you should always do your own research and question everything. Especially when it comes to what you put in or on your body. You can ask a grownup about nutrition, look foods up on the Internet or ask a teacher. Add some foods to each side of the list after you have done your research on them. You may find tricky foods that have evidence of being both helpful and harmful. This is when you need to follow your inner wisdom and make the best choices for yourself. You can always revisit the food to learn more about it.

Also, do not feel bad if you are eating many of the foods on the right side of the chart. Healthy eating is a learning process for kids and adults. It takes time to change your habits and gets easier with support. If you can, ask the grownups in your life if you can practice healthy eating together.

I used to eat ice cream for breakfast and fast

food all the time. It's been a learning process for me, too and I still have plenty to learn! There are many healthy alternatives to replace the foods you may eat that are not healthy. It takes time to adjust to new foods. You may try something and not like it. Don't give up on it. Just try one bite of the new food each time you can. It takes about 13 times or more for your body to get used to something new. If you keep trying, you may even discover a new favorite food!

An occasional treat is okay. You don't have to completely cut out the foods you enjoy. As you eat healthier foods your body will crave less of the unhealthy foods. Find the joy of fueling your body with foods that will heal you and build a healthy body. You are what you eat!

How to Build a Better Body

Eat These	Limit or Avoid These
Bananas	Hot dogs
Apples	Hamburgers
Blueberries	Chips
Raspberries	Cheese
Strawberries	Yogurt*
Grapes	Ice Cream
Avocados	Eggs
Spinach	Processed lunch meat
Celery	White bread
Cucumbers	White sugar
Arugula	French fries
Broccoli	Anything fried
Sweet potatoes	Pizza*
Nuts	Donuts
Coconut	Pancakes*
Seeds	Cookies
Wild rice	Candy
Seaweeds	

*These foods can be prepared so they are healthier, but usually grocery stores sell many unhealthy versions. For example, you can pick a yogurt made with real fruit and no added sugar, instead of a yogurt with added sugar, artificial flavors or sweeteners.

1. What are some healthy foods you eat now?_____
   _____
   _____
   _____

2. What are some foods you eat that you may want to try to limit or avoid?
   _____
   _____
   _____
   _____

3. What new foods might you try?
   _____
   _____
   _____
   _____
   _____
   _____

4. Pick one or two foods from the list on the left and find a recipe online that uses them. Make the recipe or come up with your own idea for a snack or meal. Have a grownup help you make it and share it with your family or friends.

Eat the
Rainbow

Water Is Medicine

id you know that your body and Mother Earth are both made up of 75 percent water? What a fascinating similarity that shows our connection to the planet! We know that planet Earth can support the life forms it does because it has water. That's because water itself is alive and brings energy to anything it touches. You can actually live for about three weeks without food, but only three to four days without water. Clearly, water is absolutely vital for humans to be healthy.

Entire books have been devoted to describing all the ways that water helps the body. It's that complicated and a great topic to explore further! For now, let's keep it simple. When you drink water, think of it as a river that flows through your body. It branches out, spreading everywhere. This river delivers healthy nutrients where they are needed. It also washes away toxins and garbage that are harmful to the body. This clean river keeps your body working in complete harmony. Its life force flows through your physical body, energizing every cell.

The best way to get your river flowing is to drink water! It seems so simple, and it is supposed to be. Unfortunately, many companies try to make big bucks tricking you into thinking you need other drinks. They use famous athletes or catchy slogans to sell sugary sports drinks, milk, and juices. They add tons of sugar and artificial flavors, so your body gets confused and begins to crave them. This is how the company locks you in as a customer. They pollute your river with toxins and get rich from it!

When I was little, I drank tons of milk because my parents thought it would help me grow big and strong. That's what they saw on TV, and the doctors even recommended it. I always had stomachaches after eating or drinking dairy products, but I never made the connection until I got older. As an adult, I learned that humans are the only animal that drinks the milk of another animal. Baby cows drink cow milk, then they stop when they're old enough. Baby goats drink goat milk, then they stop when they're old enough. Baby kittens drink cat milk, then they stop when they're old enough. Baby humans drink human milk, then they stop and start drinking cow milk instead. Wait, that doesn't make sense! Humans' stomachs are not designed like cows' stomachs, which have four parts. That's why many people who consume dairy (milk, cheese, yogurt, ice cream) get stomach pains and gas after they eat it. Stinky gas and bad cramps are the body's way of saying, *I do not like this stuff! No thank you.*

Keep the pollution out of your river and stick to water with some real juices or smoothies on occasion. Sadly, much of our water nowadays has been so processed that by the time it reaches our lips the life force in it is gone. Some towns even add fluoride to the water. They believe that fluoride helps prevent tooth decay. On the contrary, studies show that fluoride can be toxic to humans. It destroys the pineal gland, which is a small gland in your forehead area that helps you connect to your spiritual side. Fluoride is also added to most toothpaste, so talk to a grownup about purchasing one without it. And when the dentist wants give you fluoride treatments, do some research with a grownup to make the best choice. It's healthy to question what is done to your body, even if a doctor recommends it.

The best way to get your water is from natural sources such as a spring or a mountain. This sounds so lovely and ideal, but most of us can't make that happen. Since this isn't possible for many of us, we need other ways to put the life force back into our water. There are a few things you can do. First, you can squeeze a piece of organic lemon or lime into it, which helps return the living energy. Another idea is to leave a glass pitcher of water in the sun. This also restores its life force and makes it good for drinking. If you live in an area where your family has concerns about water quality, there are systems that can be purchased to clean up your water. You can ask your parents to look into a filtration system that helps remove any toxins that may have snuck their way in. It's a wise investment!

Now that we know what kind of water is best let us explore when to drink it! You want to drink water when you first wake up to start your river flowing. Warm water with lemon is the best! It helps flush out the digestive system and rehydrate the body after sleeping. Drink throughout the day and stay hydrated. If your pee is dark yellow it means your river is running dry. Drink more! Try to drink between meals and not while eating meals or snacks. There is hydrochloric acid in your stomach that helps break down food so your body can use the nutrients. If water is mixed with food, the acid isn't as powerful and can't do as good of a job. Finally, drink a little more water before you go to bed. Not too much, or you know what will happen. You don't want the river to flow while you are sleeping!

It's no mistake that your body is mostly made of water, just like Mother Earth. We are very much connected to our planet and made of the same elements. Just as we want to keep the sacred oceans, rivers and lakes of our world clean, we must do the same for our bodies. God created water to nourish us with the energy we need to survive on Earth.

1. What are your water drinking habits?

   _____

   _____

   _____

   _____

   _____

   _____

2. What is one goal you could set to improve
   your river?

   _____

   _____

   _____

   _____

   _____

   _____

   _____

   _____

   _____

   _____

Nature Is Medicine

*I*magine being outside on a warm day with the sun shining on your face, a gentle breeze on your skin and the birds singing. This scene, as simple as it sounds, brings us great comfort because we are meant to be in nature! Our bodies need time outside, surrounded by all Mother Earth has to offer!

Getting sunshine on your body is super important. The sun's rays are very healing and provide us with nourishing energy. Every day, you should try to get outside and allow the sun to touch your skin with no sunscreen for about

20 minutes. Allow yourself to absorb the sun's rays as a flower or plant would do! Many people are scared of the sun because they may have gotten a sunburn at one time or another. You don't have to be fearful, just be wise about your time in the sun. The sun is usually strongest in the middle of the day. You may want to wear protective clothing like a hat or apply a safe, natural sunblock if you are going to be outside for longer periods of time. If you live in a climate where it gets very cold and it's difficult to go outside, try to sit by a window that lets in sunshine. You may have to fight your cat or dog for a spot! They instinctively understand the importance of sun.

Spending time near water or surrounded by trees is also great for your soul's energy. Swimming or dipping your feet in an ocean, river or natural lake is a great way to connect with living water instead of a human made pool that might contain chemicals. You can also hike or walk on a nature trail or through a park. Instead of bringing headphones to listen to music, use your five senses to experience nature. Listen to the sounds you hear, such as birds and insects. See if you can spot some interesting animals or trees. Notice any smells or feelings you get as you explore.

If you can, spend some time barefoot in nature. It is a great way to connect your body with the energy of the earth. Try to imagine yourself as a tree. Picture roots growing out of the bottom of your feet down into the grass and dirt, strongly anchoring you. You can then imagine a swirling bright white light of energy coming up from those roots in the earth. Let it flow through your feet and slowly make its way to your head. Then picture it traveling back down through your arms, out of the palms of your hands. You may even begin to notice your body tingling as you move energy around! This is called grounding and it is very healing to the body.

If you are like most kids, you already spend a great deal of time indoors during the school day. When you get home, get outside and take in that fresh air! Your body was made to move. Enjoy a walk, run, play a game or sport, dance, or do any other exercise you prefer. Be careful about technology such as TV, videogames, cell phones and computers. These devices are meant to be fun, but they distract us and keep us from connecting to nature. They are highly addictive and lead to problems such as hyperactivity and difficulty socializing if they are overused.

Keep yourself healthy and go outside! Take in all the beauty of the land and water around you. Breathe in that fresh, healing air. There is a reason why people feel so good when they connect with Mother Earth. Start to notice how being outside affects your mood. You will be sure to give yourself a daily dose of nature once you see how great it makes you feel!

1. What are three activities you like doing outside? Why do you like them?

_____

_____

_____

2. Where do you enjoy walking or hiking? Why? _____

_____

_____

3. What inside activity can you give up to get outside more each day?

_____

_____

_____

4. Plan a nature walk with your family. Bring a backpack with water, a healthy snack and a notebook in case you want to record anything. Get out there and do it!

Sleep Is Medicine

Can you imagine only sleeping four hours over the course of five days? Maybe it sounds cool to you because you could play outside for hours, catch up on tons of movies or hang out with friends until the wee hours of the night! Some of the top soldiers of the USA, the Navy SEALS, are required to do this as part of their training. They need to stay awake for days on end and do rigorous training including running, swimming, climbing, and plunging into freezing water. Taking away their natural desire to sleep is part of the training to make them tough.

Ask your parent what it was like when you were a baby. It probably felt like Navy SEAL training! Babies don't have the same sleeping patterns that kids and adults do because they need to be up to eat every couple of hours. Parents of newborns get little sleep and it feels like torture! Most grownups will agree that sleep is a wonderful thing. Offer them a nap, and they will respond like they won the lottery.

As kids, you probably feel the opposite! It is like torture for you to go to bed. It always feels too early! You would rather stay up! You have things you want to do. If someone made you nap, you might just freak out!

When your parents are strictly enforcing your bedtime, they have some secret knowledge they learned as grownups. Most people don't realize the secrets of sleep until later in life. It usually takes a period of time when you have little sleep to really appreciate what it does for you.

When you sleep, there are many things going on in our bodies that modern science doesn't even fully understand. We do know that while we sleep our bodies use that time to get rid of toxins and repair themselves. It reminds me of staying at a hotel. When you check in, the room always looks perfect. The bed is made with freshly changed sheets, the floor is vacuumed, and the bathroom has been sanitized perfectly. But by the end of your stay it is a different story. After you've been there for a bit, the sheets are a wreck, the floor has towels and clothes all over the place, and the bathroom . . . well let's just say it's been used! Now the hotel makes you check out at 11 A.M. and won't let the next group of people go to that room until 3 P.M. They need those four hours to do some major clean up. In that time, the house-keeping staff takes away all the dirty linens and replaces them with freshly washed sheets and bedspreads. They vacuum the floors and clean the bathroom. Maintenance comes by and fixes anything that broke. By 3 P.M., that room looks new and ready to go again.

Your body does the same thing at night while you sleep. It uses the several hours of down time to clean you up and make you ready to go again. Anything your body detects as bad for you, such as viruses, bacteria, or harmful substances you ate or drank, is sent on its way. Your body produces new cells that replace any that are old or broken. It also makes new cells to help you grow bigger and stronger. This is why little babies and kids sleep longer when they are having a growth spurt. The body is working overtime!

Now, back to the hotel room. Imagine what it would look like if the staff was not given time to clean up between guests. Leftover food would begin to rot and soon bugs would show up and invite their friends. Mold would start to grow in the bathroom and it would get super smelly. It would be a disaster! Without proper sleep, you would also feel like a disaster. You might be tired, sluggish, forgetful, and moody, plus you might crave things you don't really need, like extra food.

Hopefully now you realize you had it backwards. Instead of fighting your parents to go to bed, you should be thanking them! Even begging them to go to bed earlier and sleeping later, especially on weekends! Okay, so maybe this will not happen, ever. But remember this body of yours is the only one you get, so it's helpful to know how to make it perform its best.

For peak performance toddlers need 10 to 13 hours of sleep per day, school aged kids need 9 to 11 hours, and teenagers need 8 to 10 hours. Each person is slightly different, and you will learn to gauge what you truly need to be your best.

To get a great rest, try to go to bed around the same time every night so your body knows what to expect. Create a relaxing bedtime routine for yourself. I like to take a bath, read inspiring books, and meditate before bed each night. It helps me calm my body and mind, so I fall asleep easily and wake up rested. Try to avoid eating and screen time such as TV, video games or phones a couple of hours before you sleep. They stimulate your body and mind, instead of helping you settle them down. If you struggle with sleep, you can even try some peaceful nature music, lavender spray on your pillow, or a guided meditation. Your family can support you with ideas to help you get into a solid bedtime routine.

It's pretty cool to think that your body was perfectly created with its own built-in cleaning and repair system. To activate it, all you have to do is close your eyes and allow yourself to drift into a deep sleep. Your body will automatically do the rest for you, so you can wake up feeling recharged and ready to take on the world! Sweet dreams just got a lot sweeter!

1. What is your current bedtime routine like now?_____

_____

_____

_____

_____

2. What might you change to make it even better?_____

_____

_____

_____

_____

_____

3. Using the guidelines mentioned, what time should you be going to bed in order to get the proper amount of sleep for your age?

_____

_____

Forgiveness
Is Medicine

magine going under the sink and emptying all the cleaners and dish detergents into a huge bucket. You take a giant spoon and mix up the floor cleaner, the counter sprays, the blue toilet bowl cleaner, the dusting spray and so on. Now you have a very dangerous bucket of poison. How would you like to carry this around with you for a day, a week or a lifetime? That sounds like torture. It would be super heavy and very toxic to breathe in. Also, if you spilled any, which would be bound to happen, you would get poison on you. How would you like to take a drink from it? That would clearly be a horrible idea! It would lead to major sickness or even death. (Never actually try this . . . it is only an example to help you picture a bucket of poison.)

The bad feelings we experience in our bodies like anger, rage, resentment, and jealousy are like the cleaners under the sink. We do need them sometimes, and it's okay to feel them. They can serve a purpose in our lives. They can help us gauge situations and make smart choices. But if we let them stay in our bodies for too long, they start to collect in our bucket. They weigh us down and make us feel bad. If we leave them there too long, they cause problems. It begins with the mind. Negative feelings lead to negative thoughts and actions. Eventually those bad feelings can make us physically sick!

It is very important to let go of those bad feelings and make peace within your heart. You can do this by forgiving. We forgive others because we love ourselves. We know that forgiveness allows us to take that bucket of poison and dump it out. We feel lighter, happier and relieved. When you forgive someone, you are not saying that what he or she did was acceptable. You are saying that you honor yourself enough to not carry that bucket of bad feelings around anymore.

True forgiveness takes a lot of strength. To lift that heavy bucket high and release it is no easy task. But the healing that comes after is completely worth it. One way to forgive someone is to tell him or her in person. Another way is to write it out. If you do not have the chance to see or talk to the person that hurt you, then you can still forgive him or her by sharing it with God.

Not only is it important to forgive others, but you also need to forgive yourself. We are here on this planet to learn and we all make mistakes. Sometimes our mistakes hurt others. This adds poison to our own bucket. It is wise to ask for forgiveness in person if you feel you caused someone hurt feelings or pain.

By choosing your words and actions carefully, you can aim to bring joy to others. When you forgive others and yourself you make room for peace and love in your heart.

1. Describe a time you felt hurt by another person.

_____

_____

_____

_____

_____

_____

2. Did you forgive him or her? If not, can you forgive him or her now?

_____

_____

_____

_____

_____

_____

_____

_____

Dangerous
Addictions

*H*ave you ever been painting with a lovely palette of many colors? You add a little of one color, then another, and another. It's looking really fantastic, so you add one more color and *bam*, something goes terribly wrong. All those pretty colors mixed together and made the most disgusting brown. You can't unmix the colors. The artwork is ruined. Many of us learned this when we first experimented with painting. Sometimes too much of one thing can spoil the entire thing. It sets it out of balance.

Like the painting, people can also become out of balance when they have too much of one thing.

When I was in 6th grade, we had a police officer come into our classroom to tell us about the dangers of drugs and alcohol in a program called D.A.R.E. (Drug Abuse Resistance Education). We spent weeks learning about the effects of drugs and alcohol, especially how addicting they could be. This means that when your body gets a little taste of them, it craves more and more. You begin to feel out of control like you can't live without them. I understood this feeling because I already felt this way about soda, chocolate and sweets. We had these sugary foods on the counter and I could help myself at any time. I had been eating and drinking them for years and was addicted.

Back when I was a kid, cigarettes, drugs, alcohol, and sugar were all the addictions parents were concerned about. Nowadays, the newest and most alarming danger kids face is addiction to screen time. Many kids are locked in their rooms playing with their phones, computers or video games for hours. Even schools are using computers more and more for learning. Too much technology will negatively affect you because it changes your brain and can damage the way you interact with people. It makes people spend more time alone, when we would all benefit from coming together.

Besides technology, there are many other things people can become addicted to. Addictions can range from shopping, gambling, drinking alcohol, eating too much food, and more. Usually, people become addicted to certain things because it temporarily gives them a good feeling. It distracts them from the problems they may be facing in real life.

That is why it is very important to learn to create balance in life and to follow your inner guidance. Imagine the end result before you do something. Stay away from things that will not add true joy to your life. Don't be tempted to try things that are possibly addicting like cigarettes or drugs. If you are doing something that is bringing harm to you or could bring harm to you, ask for help. Question things that don't feel right to you and make your own choices. Stopping an addiction is challenging, but it can be done. If you avoid something bad in the first place it is easier than trying to stop down the road.

It goes back to taking care of your car. When you have an addiction, it is like driving around with a popped tire. The entire car might be in perfect shape, but if your tire is blown out, you really can't go anywhere. The ride would be rough, and the car would continue to get damaged until you fix the tire. Addictions will prevent you from getting out on the road and experiencing life. God wants you to enjoy your free will, but do so with love and respect for your one physical body.

1. Have you felt out of balance because you were too involved with something?

_____

_____

_____

_____

_____

_____

2. What could you do instead that would be a better choice?_____

_____

_____

_____

_____

_____

_____

Part 4

Loving

Others

Welcome to Classroom Earth

Do you have days where you don't feel like going to school? Maybe you have even asked your parents if you could stay home because you didn't want to go. You probably groaned at them and said, "Why do I have to go?" And their response might have been, "You have to go to school to learn." Whether you like school or not, you know school is supposed to teach you things that are going to help you in life. Some days in school will be filled with fun and joy, while other days may feel dreadful.

In the same way, planet Earth is like a giant classroom. We are all here to have a variety of experiences that lead to a kaleidoscope of feelings. It is through these different feelings we experience the world and decide what we prefer. While many days here in "Earth School" are fun and enjoyable, other days are downright difficult. You may feel like you are on a roller coaster riding the ups and downs of life.

Tough times are when you deal with people or events that make you sad, uncomfortable or angry. These are a necessary part of your experience on Earth. Without the storms, you wouldn't understand the sunshine. One thing you can count on is change! If you can learn to stay positive on the dark stormy days and focus on God's unconditional love, you can ride through any storm. It will always pass and the skies will clear up.

Many times after a storm, you will see a rainbow. It's amazing that something so beautiful can appear after

such bad weather. Think of the rainbow as your lesson from the challenging time in your life. Use that rainbow, or lesson, to bring beauty and joy to your future.

In the way school is separated into grades, with each grade getting more advanced, people learn at different levels in classroom Earth. You might think that as people get older, they should get smarter. But this is not always the case. Have you ever noticed an adult making a bad choice? You might shake your head and wonder how this could be since this person is a grownup. Shouldn't he or she know better?

Just remember that some people you meet will be in "kindergarten" here on Earth! This does not mean they are five-year-olds working on learning the alphabet. Being in kindergarten just means that some people have lots to learn and sometimes make choices that aren't the best. Try not to judge them, but instead send them positive thoughts of love to help them move on to "first grade"!

Other people you meet will be so wise and

will have great knowledge to share with you. These people are the college kids of life in Earth School. Surround yourself with them and you will grow from their wisdom.

So, welcome to your big swirly blue and green ball of a classroom! This is your chance to learn and grow. Take in all of these experiences. Instead of judging any as right or wrong, or good or bad, be grateful for them all. Always remember God is with you through all the ups and downs on this journey. You are never alone.

1. What was a challenging time you experienced recently? _____

_____

_____

_____

_____

2. What did you learn from that experience?

_____

_____

_____

_____

_____

3. How might that experience help you in the future?

_____

_____

_____

_____

_____

Everyone
Is a Teacher

f life is our classroom, each day we can expect to learn some lessons. The people we encounter are going to be our teachers. Each person is so uniquely different. This creates many opportunities to learn! It is up to us, the students, to figure out the lesson and let it change us for the better. Some people will come into our lives for a long time and others for a short time. Some people will come into our lives and make us feel great and others will make us feel bad. It doesn't matter, there are always lessons to be learned. Classroom Earth is filled with teachers. You are also one!

One of my greatest lessons came from a coworker in my school when I was teaching fifth grade. Unfortunately, I could tell she didn't like me. I felt uncomfortable when I saw her or had to speak with her at school. Fortunately, I loved being a teacher and I imagined myself in a classroom until I was old.

After I gave birth to my first son, I had intended to come back to my classroom, but I knew it was not healthy to be in a situation where I felt bullied by this coworker. I decided to stay home with my son and take the year off.

In that time, I had the most magical year of my life. I enjoyed every minute of time with my baby boy and saw so many firsts I would have missed. I started two small businesses that allowed me to work part time, still doing what I loved. After a year of this lifestyle, I was not ready to go back to the classroom. I felt I had shifted and was right where I belonged!

When I think back to that coworker, I am forever grateful for her lessons. At the time, her behavior toward me was painful and confusing, but now I see she was just a teacher. If it wasn't for her I would have never left the classroom. I wouldn't have started my own company. And I wouldn't have written this book. She came into my life for a purpose. From her I learned to take care of myself and honor my wellbeing. I learned that change is healthy. I learned I didn't need to have a plan, I could let life unfold. Those were awesome lessons I would need in my future to help me be my best.

You will encounter many teachers in your life. People of all ages, shapes, colors, sizes, cultures, and backgrounds will challenge you for better or worse. Some you will like more than others. Some will show you what to do, others will show you what not to do. Just remember that each person offers valuable lessons to be learned. When you approach life with that in mind, you will really begin to appreciate people's

differences. The more you honor those differences, the stronger you will feel connected to
all those you meet.

1. Name any person in your life. What is one lesson that person taught you?

_____

_____

_____

_____

_____

_____

2. Think about a main character in a recent book you've read or movie you've watched. What lesson can you learn from that person?

_____

_____

_____

_____

_____

_____

_____

23

Giving from the Heart

Have you noticed that we live in a world of opposites? Good and bad, dark and light, up and down, hot and cold, happy and sad. These contrasting ideas help us understand our world and make sense of it. Without both extremes, we couldn't compare things or categorize them. Contrast also helps us appreciate things. I live in a state that has four seasons and when it's winter, all I think about is the warm summer sun that will be coming. I appreciate summer more because I have winter to compare it to!

As soon as you were born, your parents began to teach you about another pair of opposites that are extremely important. They poured into you. They guided every moment of your early journey. Your parents gave you food, drinks, and attention. As a baby, you took it all in. Babies are great little receivers, taking, and taking. They are not capable of giving much back yet.

As you got a bit older, you most likely began to understand the joy of giving. Reaching your arms out for a snuggle or uttering an unprompted, "I love you," would melt your parents' hearts. You may have drawn a picture and given it away. Even a few scribbles, when given with love, become a treasure. These little moments are the first gifts you offer back after being a receiver for years! This is your introduction to the law of giving and receiving, a magical pair of opposites we have on Earth.

One of the many reasons we are here in classroom Earth is to serve others. Serving simply means bringing true joy to others. The way we serve others looks very different depending upon our unique gifts, resources, and choices. There are many ways to serve, but it always involves giving. Luckily, you have endless gifts to give others.

When we think of gifts, we typically imagine giving someone a physical gift. A physical gift is anything that can be touched, including money. We can give others a physical gift they may need or want. I personally like to give my family gifts at holidays or birthdays. I also like to give money to my church and other organizations that I feel add value to peoples' lives.

Sometimes I bring clothes to an organization in my town that gives them away to people in need. These gifts are called donations. You give them away with no expectation of anything in return. You know you are bringing joy to others, which in turn brings joy to you! We feel joy when we do this because we are activating the law of giving and receiving. One flows into the other. When we give, we open the door to receive. What we receive back will vary.

When my son was seven, we spent the afternoon collecting items to donate to a local charity. We delivered hundreds of dollars worth of clothes and home goods. Later that evening, we went to our first BMX bike practice. We saw our neighbors there we had recently met. They gave us very valuable sporting equipment that their kids had outgrown for free. These were items I would have needed to buy in the next week. They saved me tons of money and our hearts were filled with gratitude. The law of giving and receiving was very obvious that day!

Besides physical things, we also give our

time and energy when we do things for another person or for our community. Maybe you do a chore without being asked or you volunteer to help clean up your local park. Both are ways you are using your time and energy to bring joy to others. Think about each person in your family. What is one thing you could do that would be a gift for them? It is the best when you do something helpful without being asked. Give it a try and watch the joy you will create in your home!

Another way to give to others is to use your words. Kind words that lift others up are truly a gift. They are free and easy to give away! You never know if your inspiring words will change the course of someone's life. Make your compliment specific and honest.

One of the best compliments I ever received came from a mom of a student in my class. We were on a bus returning from a field trip, and I was explaining that I would be leaving teaching for a year and starting my own tutoring company. She told me I was going to be great at it. She said that no matter what I did in life, I would always be successful at it because that's the way I am. Those words burned into my heart forever. Anytime I face a new challenge, I open the treasure box in my mind and hear those words. They are like precious gem stones I can keep with me when I need an emotional lift!

You can start today using your words, time and resources to bring joy to others. Give with all your heart and with no expectation to receive anything back. God will provide you with everything you need, so do not stress that you will not have enough. Have faith that you will open the door to receiving when you allow yourself to give freely and generously.

1. What is one thing or service you could give to a family member?_____

   _____

   _____

   _____

   _____

   _____

2. What is one thing you could say to a family member or friend that would be a gift?

   _____

   _____

   _____

   _____

   _____

   _____

3. Create a banking system for yourself. Use three separate jars or envelopes. Label one *Giving*, one *Savings*, and one *Spending*. When you get money, talk with your parents how to best divide it up into your different categories. Enjoy sharing your *giving* money with someone or something you feel passionately about. Enjoy the *spending* money to purchase things you want. Money in the *saving* category can be collected for something major you want in your future. Maybe it could be used to pay for college or to buy a car. Let it sit there and pile up or ask your parents to put it in an account that earns interest, or bonus money. See if you can avoid touching it until it's time to make your big purchase.

Seeking Wisdom

Not long ago, many people thought it was okay to keep children with black skin away from children with white skin. Children with black skin were put in different schools with fewer supplies, had to use different water fountains, and were forced to sit in the backs of buses. The color of people's skin determined how they were treated. People with white skin were viewed as better and smarter than people with black skin. Of course, people with white skin are not smarter than people with black skin and all people deserve to be treated equally. This may seem ridiculous that a person's skin color could affect so much. How could people have allowed this to happen? For many people that lived in this time, it was considered "normal" to treat people with black skin poorly. People usually don't question what is "normal". But sometimes, what we learn is "normal" needs to be questioned and changed!

From a very early age, your parents and family members begin to teach you everything they can. This shapes how you see the world. We all come into this world like a perfect lump of clay. Everything our family and friends say and do molds our clay and shapes us. We develop strong likes and dislikes, many times based on other people's opinions. I remember talking to my nephew when he was in elementary school. He told me he hated airplanes and didn't want to fly. He had never been on an airplane! I asked him why he felt that way. He told me his dad hated heights and thought they were scary, so he felt the same way, too.

We love and trust our family and friends to

guide us and give us good information and positive experiences. Most times they mean well and have our best interests in mind as they guide us. But you have to remember that they are human, and no human is perfect. Therefore, it is impossible for them to know everything. They will develop their own opinions on things and have their own set of likes and dislikes. Your job is to listen and consider any ideas presented to you, but to find your own truth.

God has equipped you with a brain that is super intelligent. Your learning mode can be activated at any time. Sources such as people, books, the Internet, and your experiences can give you information. Your heart and your gut, a feeling in your belly, help guide you to your own understanding of life. Real wisdom comes from exploring an area using many resources. Take from those resources what feels right to you.

Question everything. Be very careful about what you view as normal. Do not accept the way things are right at this moment as normal. If something feels wrong or weird then ask about it and work to change it. Recently, my son asked me why the cafeteria at school serves kids cinnamon buns for breakfast before school. He knows they are sugary and lack real nutrition. He said, "Wouldn't a breakfast like that make it hard for a kid to learn all day if they feel crummy?" My response was, "Yes, it's a horrible choice for kids to eat, so why do they do it and what can you do about it?"

One of your missions in life is to leave this world a better place than you found it. So while you are here on classroom Earth, learn, learn, learn! Don't save your learning just for the school day, always seek wisdom and question what you notice! God created you to be a thinking being who is powerful and wise. Respect others who want to teach you, but do not accept all they share as true. Seek your own truth and make this world a better place.

1. What is something you'd like to learn more about? _____

_____

_____

2. What are some ways you could learn about it?

_____

_____

_____

3. Describe something many people may consider normal, but that you don't agree with.

_____

_____

_____

_____

_____

_____

_____

The Bully Brain

There is one in every class. The kid every-one is scared of because he's a ticking time bomb. You never know when he is going to do something nasty, but you know it's coming. He may hit kids and say awful things to their faces or behind their backs. This kid makes everyone uncomfortable! Some kids may even join in on the nastiness by laughing or following along to avoid being targeted. You try to avoid this kid at all costs, but sometimes you do have an en-counter with . . . the bully. When I was younger, I struggled with the question, "What is going on inside that bully's brain?" Then I got an answer I didn't expect.

I knew one of these "mean" girls when I was in elementary school. She would say rude things about me when I was nearby. She'd look at me and giggle, then whisper to her friend something obviously about me. She even tried to steal my best friend, so I didn't have anyone to play with. She hurt my heart.

One day I was telling my older cousin about her and she said something that shocked me. It forever changed the way I thought about this bully. She told me this girl was probably mean because people were most likely mean to her at home. Maybe her home life wasn't so good. My cousin suggested I should try to feel compassion for her instead of anger.

I gave my cousin a crazy look. "You want me to love this bully?" I said in disbelief. "Yup." She told me the girl probably needed love in her life. That's when it hit me. I started to imagine all the possibilities of life someone could experience once they left school and went home.

Did her parents hit her? Did they swear at her? Did they not spend quality time with her? Maybe they drank too much alcohol or used drugs? Of course, she may even have had a perfectly fine home life! But it opened my eyes. I realized that kids who bully others probably have troubles of their own and are struggling to deal with their issues.

From that day on, I had a whole new perspective. I knew I couldn't control anyone else's behaviors, but I could change my reaction to them. Now when I encountered bullies my first thought would be, "I wonder what troubles they are dealing with in life?" This helped me view them with compassion and have more patience for them. It didn't mean I agreed with how they acted or that I had to be their friend. It just gave me a chance to view them through a new pair of glasses. God wears similar glasses. These glasses see the good in all people and know that love solves most problems.

The next time you encounter a bully, pause for a moment before reacting. Involve a grownup if needed, because your safety is very important. There are many people who love you and can help you. Next, reflect on all the blessings in your own life and feel grateful. These are joys the bully may not have. Then try to send him or her thoughts or words that show compassion and love. We have learned how our words and thoughts can heal. Not only can they work for our own bodies, but they can also help others. This is what bullies need the most; to have their hearts healed.

1. Have you been bullied before? If not, have you seen someone else get bullied? Tell about what happened. _____

    _____

    _____

    _____

    _____

    _____

2. Did you think about why the kid acted like a bully? Have your thoughts changed at all? If so, explain._____

    _____

    _____

    _____

    _____

    _____

    _____

3. Is there a time when your words or actions could have made someone feel bullied? If so, think about how you made the other person feel. _____

_____

_____

_____

_____

_____

_____

_____

_____

_____

_____

_____

_____

Choosing
Friends

Did you know you become similar to the five people you hang out with the most? That means you better pick those five people carefully. While you are young, you have little control when it comes to spending time with your family. I hope they are a positive influence on you and give you many blessings. Fortunately, you do have a choice of whom you pick for friends and you should choose wisely.

Before we talk about finding great friends, we need to explore being an amazing friend. When

you work hard to be a great friend you will attract great friends into your life. Here are some
ways to be a fabulous friend.

Rules for Being a Fabulous Friend

1. Be a good listener. When someone is talking to you, look at him in the eyes and stay focused on the words you hear. Ask questions to learn more about what he is telling you. People like to talk about themselves and when you are interested in what they have to say it builds your connection.

2. Be a good talker. Tell a friend about your life. Being open and honest helps you form connections with them. Be sure to give her a chance to talk too, so the conversation isn't all about you. There should be a balance.

3. Be a helper. See how you can lend a hand to a friend. Offer caring advice if he is feeling down, or offer to help with a project or schoolwork if he needs it. Giving up some of your time to provide a service is an act of love.

4. Be trustworthy and respectful. If a friend tells you something private, do not share it unless she says it's okay or you feel she is not safe. Never talk about a friend badly when she isn't around. This is called gossiping and it is very hurtful.

5. Be encouraging with your words. When you speak to your friend, try to be positive and kind. We all enjoy hearing compliments and uplifting words. People won't want to be around you if you are always complaining, bragging or being negative.

6. Be giving. We all feel good when someone gives us something. A small item or a handwritten letter can mean a lot to a person.

7. Be willing to spend time together. Friendships develop when you invest your most precious resource, which is your time. Play or go somewhere together. Quality time will strengthen your friendship.

We all have different areas of strength. For example, some of us are good listeners, while others are very giving. Think about how you are already a good friend. What do you do that makes others want to be friends with you? What area might you want to improve in?

Being a good friend is something you have the ability to control and improve upon. You can also choose who you'd like to be friends with. There is a big difference between being friendly and having a good friend. You should try to be friendly and kind to all people, but that doesn't mean you have to be friends with them. The friends you pick should be people who make you feel good in your heart. They should have qualities you admire. You should feel special when you're with them.

Some friends that you have when you are young may turn out to be lifelong friends. But many friends will only be in your life for a short time. Do not feel upset if you had a good friend but grew apart from him or her. You needed each other in your life for that season, but then it was time to move on. If a friend hurts you badly, you will need to decide if it's time to end that friendship or forgive him or her and continue to be friends. Keep in mind that a friend who is frequently hurting you is not really a true friend. It's better to let that person go and make room in your heart for other friends.

Always stay open to making new friends. Along your Earth journey, you will have many friendships. You will meet different people every year and each person you meet could be a potential new friend. It's a great way to view each person you encounter. We were meant to go through life together. That is why God surrounded us with people. Be the best friend you can to others, and you will attract great friends into your life.

1. Who is one of your good friends? Why do you like him or her? _____

_____

_____

_____

_____

2. What qualities make you a good friend?

_____

_____

_____

_____

_____

3. What qualities do you want in a friend?

_____

_____

_____

_____

_____

27

Saying
See You Later

When I was in elementary school, it was cool to have pet hermit crabs. They came in small plastic containers with brightly colored lids and a handle to carry them around. I remember picking neon pink rocks for the floor of my tank and decorating it with beautifully colored shells. My first hermit crab had a speckled green and brown shell. The opening of the shell had been dipped in gold paint. I felt so proud that my crab had such a luxurious place to call home. Every day I fed him and gave him clean water. He didn't do much except crawl around, but I enjoyed taking him out. I was so curious to see his entire body without the shell, but he never fully came out while I was around. One morning, I went in to check on him and I picked up his shell. My heart sank. He wasn't in it. Overnight, he had crawled into a new shell. I had a few extras in the tank to pick from that were larger. He must have sensed it was time to upgrade to a bigger one. It was cool to see him in his new shell. I felt proud that he was growing and that I was able to provide him with his new digs.

A human's physical body is like the shell of a hermit crab. When we die, we leave our bodies behind like empty shells we have outgrown.

When my dad died, I remembered my heart dropped like it did when my crab was gone from his shell, only this time, my heart dropped even harder. It hurt to see the empty shell of my dad's body. But just like a hermit crab was more than an empty shell, I felt that inside my dad's body there had been something more . . . his soul. It had not died. It was perfectly fine. His soul had only left its shell and headed "home" to rest and recharge from all its growth on Earth. And just like my crab picked a new shell, I feel that some-day my dad will pick a new shell and come back for another Earth journey. His new shell will be unique and look nothing like his last one. But his soul will remain the same, just more evolved from its journey.

Death may feel like a scary topic to talk about because we do not have all the answers about what happens. This is only one opinion and you are always invited to learn others. What appears as the end of one chapter, I believe is the immediate beginning of a new one. Death is much harder for those left behind on Earth than for those who die, because we miss the physi-cal presence of our loved ones. We want to see them, talk with them, and spend time together. But for the ones leaving their shell behind, it's quite peaceful. They no longer have to carry the weight of that shell around. They feel at home, free, healthy and loved. They are still with us, and they have abilities we can't understand with our earthly minds. People who have had near death experiences have confirmed that when they left their physical bodies, they were so blissfully happy. They didn't want to return to their "shell" on Earth. They saw sights, colors, and sounds and met people that we don't even have the words to describe.

God wants you take comfort in the fact that you are eternal, which means that you live on forever. It may not be in the way you imagined, but it is true. It is in a way so amazing and wonderful that we cannot begin to understand it with our earthly minds. So when it's time to say goodbye to a loved one, instead say see you later and talk to you soon. They will still be a part of your life as their soul lives on in spirit form.

1. Do you have any loved ones in spirit?

_____

_____

_____

_____

_____

_____

_____

2. Have you ever felt they are with you or have you received a sign from them?

_____

_____

_____

_____

_____

_____

_____

_____

Understanding
Your Purpose

The older I get the more I learn, and the more I learn, the more questions I have about what I am learning. Every time I think I have discovered an answer, it usually leads to a handful of new questions I want to explore. The more I know, the more I realize how much I don't know. Real wisdom is knowing that you don't know much. It sounds silly, but it's true.

I used to imagine what it would be like to be an ant and see the world from its eyes. It's fun to try. As you read the description, try to picture it in your head. Your world is your ant hill with fellow ants. Life is good, and your ant hill is all you know. Imagine now that you are lifted out of that ant hill and you see that the land goes far beyond your ant hill. You see a house and marvel at what it could be. Imagine how long it would take you to explore every room in that house to really understand it. You couldn't do it in your ant lifetime. Now, imagine you're lifted up higher, and you see that the house is part of a town. Think about how mind blowing it would be for the ant to understand the idea that all the houses are connected by streets. Near the houses there are other places too, where people work, buy things, learn, and more. By now, your ant brain would be ready to explode. It's just too much to take in. We haven't even scratched the surface yet. We haven't shown the ant that we are in a state that is part of a country on a continent that is on planet Earth.

Many times, I feel like an ant, trying to make sense of the vast world around me. Perhaps we are all ants, trying to learn and make sense of our current world from our little ant perspective. Just like the ants can't see far beyond their hill, it's hard for us to make sense of the vast world beyond our backyards. For us, thinking about the spiritual world would be like the ant thinking about the whole planet Earth – we can't see it or wrap our heads around it.

One of the most important questions that we ask as humans is why are we here? What are we supposed to do here? Some people call this trying to understand our soul's purpose. It is a great question, and there are even thousands of books that spend hundreds of pages trying to answer it. I will try to answer it in one single paragraph.

The part of us that is everlasting, our spirit, chose to come here. It's not always fun and happy on Earth, so the rewards of coming must be important. There must be things that we cannot experience while in spirit form, so we come here to do so in physical form. If you were a flashlight next to the sun, you couldn't experience your light because there was only light. But if I put you in total darkness, your light would be obvious. We need contrast to understand our world. Therefore, both light and dark are important. One is not better than the other; they just are what they are. It is through these contrasts in life that we can have experiences on Earth. We can use the feelings they create to understand our likes and dislikes. Then we can seek more or less of them. In this way we decide who we want to be and create ourselves. You are a Creator!

This answer will probably only lead to more questions for you. And that is just perfect! Do your best to be okay with not having all the answers. Allow yourself to enjoy the mystery! God will guide you on this adventure through your feelings. You have your lifetime to explore the world we live in and remember who you are and choose who you wish to be!

Create the story of you!

1. Name a famous person you know a lot about. What do you think they may have come to Earth to do or learn?

_____

_____

_____

_____

_____

2. Interview a few grandparents or older adults. Ask them to tell you about some of the most important lessons they have learned in life.

_____

_____

_____

_____

_____

_____

End Note

Dear Loves,

Thank you for taking this journey with me. I hope you realize how magical you truly are! I am so very proud of you for reading a book to empower you to be your best version! Now that you have learned many lessons on how to be healthy and happy, it's time to put your wisdom into practice. Keep this book with you as a guide so you can come back to it as needed to refresh your memory. Always remember you are a masterpiece, loved and created by God. You have the ability to keep your body and mind healthy. You don't have to fit into the world you see. Instead, you can use your powers to create the world you want to be in! I wish you all the best on your Earth journey.

Love,
Ms. Becky

Note To Parents

Dear Parents,

The desire to write this book started as a small flame years ago when I was a teacher in a fifth grade public school classroom. I had been an upper elementary school teacher for seven years and I truly loved working with my students. I taught all subjects including reading, writing, math, social studies and science. But my real passion was teaching in the spaces between. It was the moments when their hearts expanded, their unique passions were piqued, and their trials became their most essential lessons that brought me true joy. The subjects were secondary; there was much more my kids needed to learn in order to be successful and happy.

When I gave birth to my first son I left the classroom to focus on being a mom. I still longed to connect with children and make a difference, so I started a tutoring company. In the years that followed, I had the honor of working with children from kindergarten to twelfth grade. Again, I enjoyed being with the children, but found myself disheartened by the material I was supposed to teach. I always asked myself if this would serve them in life or if it was just to get them an acceptable letter score on a report card. Too often as a society we don't question what our children are learning.

I witnessed over and over again beautiful children with innocent souls becoming frustrated and bitter because they didn't fit into the box of public school. I saw each child as a masterpiece and loved to highlight each one's unique gifts. Every child I worked with had areas of brilliance, which always became stronger with the proper encouragement. But since their gifts usually didn't fit into a school subject they felt discouraged, unmotivated and stupid. It broke my heart.

Finally, after having my own children, my calling to write this book turned into a full-blown fire. As a mom, I totally can relate to how quickly our good intentions for being a stellar parent and teaching our kids all the valuable life lessons can get lost in the shuffle. Between brushing teeth, packing lunches, giving baths, helping with homework, driving to after school activities, making dinner and putting them to bed, our energy is spent. At 8 p.m. we prep our coffee mug for the morning and pray our children will all sleep through the night, so we can function well enough to get up and do it again tomorrow.

Then there is that moment of stillness when we stop, and ask ourselves, are we missing the whole point. Did we have time to connect with our children today? Did we have time to process the day and talk about our experiences? Did we even find joy today? I have had many of these moments as a mom of three. It is in the chaos that God speaks to us and reminds us to slow down, be present, and teach our children what they need to know. We cannot depend on the school system to instill the most important lessons.

We are given our children as a gift. They are on loan to us and we have a tremendous responsibility to pour into them all the love and wisdom we hold in our cup. This book will help fill your cup. I will empower you to teach your children some valuable life lessons. I hope to restore your passion to parent with a fresh lens, knowing that you have been chosen to do the most important work.

When I wrote this book, it was my intention it would be shared as a read aloud. It is your choice how you share it with your child. It can also be read independently. If you choose to share this book with your child as a read aloud know you are about to embark upon a journey with your child. These chapters will challenge you both as they shift your view of life and bring up more questions. It is recommended to pick one chapter at a time to read with your child. Snuggle up in a comfortable place where he or she feels safe and relaxed. Try to make sure you are in a quiet space with no distractions, so your child's mind can be focused as you read and converse. Pause as often as you'd like to ask your child what he or she is thinking and to share your thoughts as well. The more interactive you are with this book the more meaning your child will gain from the lessons. You can read the chapters in order or skip around as you feel called to explore certain topics. At the end of each chapter take some time to use the questions and activities to reflect upon the ideas presented. Take what you will from each chapter and discard what does not work for you.

You are about to give your child a gift. Your time, love and guidance as you both explore your spirituality. I hope you enjoy the messages shared and come back to them as needed to encourage your child. Many blessings to you and your beautiful child.

 With love,
Becky

About the Author

*B*ecky Cummings is an author, teacher, and mom of three. She loves kids and speaking her truth. Becky is blessed to combine these passions by writing children's books that spread messages of love, hope, faith, health, and happiness. When she isn't writing you might find her salsa dancing, eating a veggie burrito at her favorite Mexican joint, or traveling to new places!

Becky is available for author visits and wants to connect with you. Be sure to visit her on Facebook, Instagram, or her website, **www.authorbcummings.com**.